ZENSHO W. KOPP

The power of inner quietude

In the depths of the heart, in our innermost self, there shines a brilliant light that lights up the whole universe like an eternal flame.

The eternally radiating light of the One Mind is our original, true self. It is completely independent of the various ways in which things appear in the realm of space and time and their myriad forms of existence.

Zen fosters absolute trust in a person's true essence and opens their inner eye to the great mystery of their Universal Essence.

When you reach complete realisation, you experience nothing other than the omnipresent buddha-being, which was with you the whole time, without interruption, as the silent observer behind all experiences.

Your thinking creates the notion of time, yet pure awareness, now-here, is beyond all transformation.

Your true being only reveals itself in inner silence. Pure being, just as it is, only reveals itself when you have become inwardly silent.

When the radiating light of the mind shines forth, you recognise yourself in your timeless eternity.

In the depths of your heart there is no division between you and divine reality. Here, you are united with the Absolute.

The experience of this unity is the revelation of that which you have always been, are now and will eternally be.

When you recognise that the reality of divine being is pure love, you experience yourself as One with all beings.

Pure love in the form of being is the love of all-embracing wholeness, which contains everything within itself.

Meditation is not a question of doing, for your true being is meditation.

Turn your mind around and behold your true self behind all thinking and feeling.

The moment you recognise your true being, your mind will pervade the entire universe.

The liberation from habitual thinking can only take place in the absolute presence of Here and Now.

When you abide in the direct moment of Now, you recollect the original state of the mind.

In pure self-awareness of the mind, your mind pervades the entire universe.

Zen is about experiencing the spiritual clarity gained both in the silence of meditation and in resting in the inner ground of being in the midst of the world and also during our daily activities.

Therefore, be completely present right here and now and live out of the fullness of the moment.

Life is too short to be spent in mindless routine and indifferent ignorance.

The experience of our true essence is the great turning point in a person's life.

It is a tremendous baptism by fire of the mind that floods our hearts with the boundless love of divine being.

When we are liberated from all concepts, we enter into the boundless joy of being.

Your true being is immortality beyond space and time.

However, your experience of past, present and future is as fleeting as a leaf blown past your window on the autumn wind.

Let go of the notion of a personal self and perceive your birthless and deathless true self.

Since the ego-concept is just an illusion, the mind can only dissolve this illusion when it turns inwards and returns to its original source and thus flourishes in its original condition.

Reality is quintessential in each instant, just as it is. There is only one, single essence and thus only one, sole self, as the sole reality of the One Mind.

Here-now! In this instant, right there where you are, reality reveals itself. You can only experience your true self in Now.

The only way to immortality is to awaken from the ego-induced dream of birth, aging, despair, illness, pain and death.

It is a great mistake to believe that we were born and will one day die, and that there is a multitude of beings and things.

Everything is just a dream, without any reality.

Zen consciousness is a pure, crystal-clear state of mind in which only the directness of the present moment exists and nothing else.

Each instant is just a fleeting moment in the consciousness.

Yet in crystal-clear awareness of mind,
Now becomes eternity.

Behind your discriminating thinking, your true being shines with undiminished clarity. It is constantly present and is covered only by your thoughts.

Why seek externally for that which is constantly present in our innermost heart-lotus as our own radiating jewel?

There is no personality that is different from other individual personalities. All waves on the ocean are the one ocean and thus everything is the One Mind, beside which nothing else exists.

Everything is the One without second in its all-encompassing wholeness.

If you wish to experience your true essence, you must put all your effort into turning inwards.

By breaking through to your true being you are raised above all limitations of an earth-bound human existence and you experience your ascent above the dark mists of pheno-mena into the clear light of reality.

The profound secret of your true being reveals itself at the very core of your heart.

The radiating, all-penetrating light of the One Mind and the infinite silence have not been interrupted in all eternity.

This light is entirely present in each person, yet people turn away from it due to their spiritual blindness.

An instant of crystal-clear awareness in your mind is the manifestation of the buddha nature within you.

Your true essence is pure being, absolute awareness and boundless bliss. Since it is the source of all joy, there is no greater joy than to perceive your true self.

Through spiritual clarity you find your way to inner silence.

Allow your mind to be vast, open and clear and let it flow freely, without dwelling on anything. This is how you melt with the essential and achieve indwelling wisdom.

When you are identified with your body and your ego, you experience the world as separate and outside of you. However, when you perceive your true self, you experience everything as an indivisible reality.

It is only your subjective mind that is attached and bound to body, mind and world.

You are liberated as soon as the ego-delusion is wiped out.

The true self is the self-illuminating essence, resting in itself, in which all things are contained.

The truth you are seeking is within you and at the same time reveals itself in all phenomena.

When you have found your way back to your original nature, your feeling of separateness ceases and you are in a state of great peace.

True bliss begins where the ego-delusion ceases to exist.

It is not possible to behold divine reality and at the same time cling to the notion of the ego. In this liberating experience there is neither perceiver, nor perception, nor the perceived.

Everything dissolves in the radiating splendour of pure being.

The ego-notion causes discriminating thinking and consequently a myriad of problems to arise.

When the mind becomes silent and clear, everything comes to rest and you abide in enduring peace. In pure, crystal-clear self-awareness of the mind there is neither I nor you, and you experience everything as the one reality.

Let your mind sink into the unfathomable depths of your true being, which intellect and thinking can never reach.

When your mind is free of thoughts and immersed in itself in complete peace and clarity, the light of the true self radiates forth in your heart as the Kingdom of God.

True spiritual realisation is when your consciousness is firmly rooted in self-awareness of mind, everywhere and at all times.

Achieve an unswerving inner certitude that you, in your true essence, are the unfading, eternal self.

Our entire experience of the world is nothing more than a dream, without any reality, and this is also true of the dreamer. Everything is just an illusory spectacle.

There are no external phenomena which are not the mind. They are like reflections and just a game of the mind. If you take them to be real, you will be deceived by them.

The splendour of divine being is constantly present, silent and pure and manifests itself as silent, mysterious, peaceful joy.

You can only find the reality of your true self within you. Everything flows from your own heart.

Zen is about achieving a state of consciousness of constant, crystal-clear self-awareness in all that you do.

In this absolute awareness of Here and Now, you recognise that the present moment is eternal.

When you give your full attention to all of your daily activities, each moment becomes meaningful and precious.

When you allow your mind to abide in intentionless self-awareness, you experience non-dualistic, original consciousness.

This pure, effortless awareness of mind is the original condition of your mind, which you do not need to achieve but just let happen.

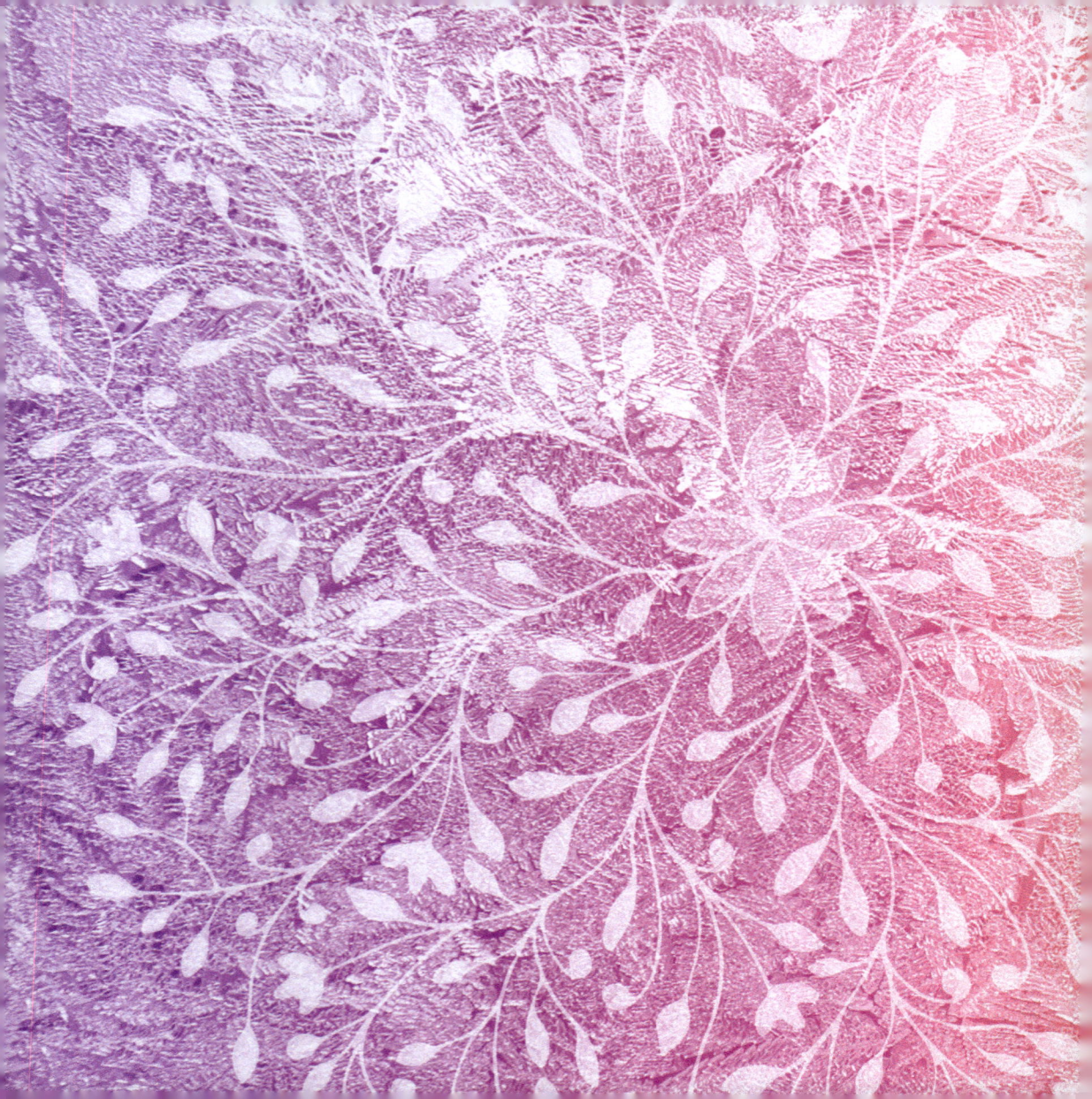

Good and bad karma depend solely on your attachment to your concepts. If you would constantly act without ego-attachment, no further negative karma could accumulate.

When the ego-notion completely ceases to exist, boundless consciousness remains that reveals itself as pure, absolute being.

The ultimate purpose of your life is to perceive yourself and to realise your true, immortal essence.

An ignorant person restricts their existence to their body and the ego-delusion. However, a person who has awakened to the reality of their true self experiences themselves as the one, all-embracing universal consciousness.

Bondage and liberation only exist in the thoughts of an ignorant person. The true self is eternally free of all duality and is the sole reality.

A person who has awakened to reality is constantly aware of their unity with highest reality. They unceasingly enjoy the ever-lasting joy of their true self.

Your true being is the reality in everything and makes all things apparent. It is the highest of all, the eternal original source of all being, the One without second.

Therefore, turn the light of spiritual awareness back to the original source of your true essence that is pure joy and bliss.

The distractions of the mind are eradicated by the power of meditation and you experience a boundless, empty consciousness beyond all thinking that is your true, immortal self.

When your mind becomes silent and the flow of thoughts suddenly dissolves in crystal-clear consciousness, the original state of your mind reveals itself, which is peace and blissful being.

The perfection of realisation is the experience of the true essence of your own mind at your deepest depths.

True perfection is a boundless ocean of wisdom. However, non-perception causes baleful confusion and endless suffering.

True prayer is wordless, devout immersion in your inner, divine ground.

The more you turn to the divine, filled with loving desire, the more you inwardly detach yourself from all things and are elevated towards God.

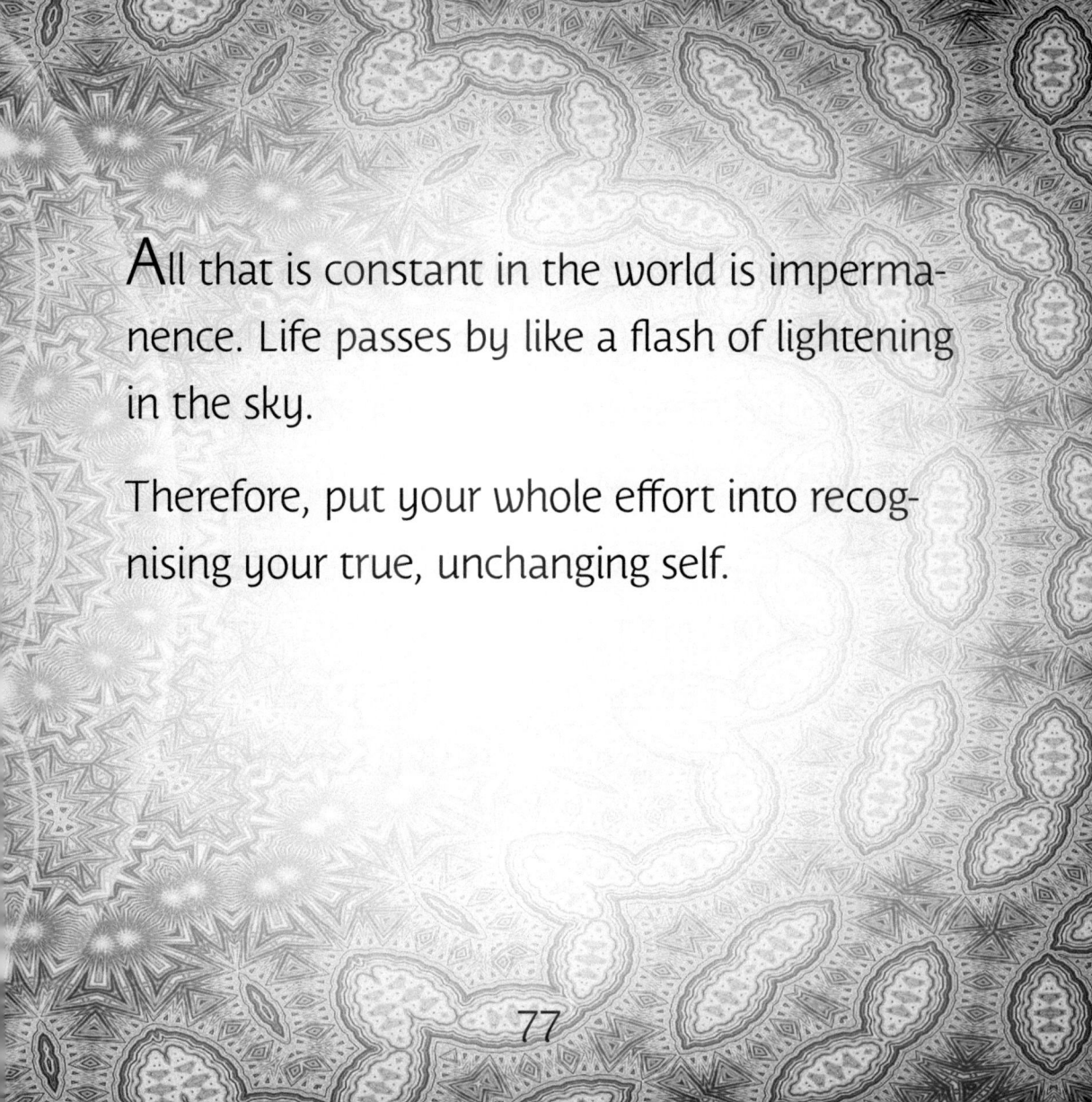

All that is constant in the world is imperma-
nence. Life passes by like a flash of lightening
in the sky.

Therefore, put your whole effort into recog-
nising your true, unchanging self.

To experience highest truth you must liberate your mind from all wanting and rejecting so that you become empty and recognise that you are one with God.

The mystery of immortality can only be fathomed by a person of pure heart who immerses themselves in their innermost self and recognises: oneness with God is immortality.

Continual self-awareness leads to inner silence. Great peace and bliss manifest themselves in this power of inner silence.

Take the sword of crystal-clear awareness and shatter every duality.

Let your thoughts just abide with what you are currently doing, without straying into the past or the future.

Spiritual eroticism is a harmony of souls and only possible by realising a meditative consciousness.

True love means being in unison and harmony with the other person.

When you are filled with divine love, you are in harmony with all beings and with the all-embracing wholeness of being.

The sage, who has achieved consummate perception of his true essence, is filled with inner bliss and is the unrestricted ruler of his thinking.

He experiences the world as existing solely of consciousness and thus he is constantly aware of his universality. He sees the whole universe as the space of his own consciousness.

Leave your mind in effortless, relaxed intentionlessness and view all arising thoughts with undistracted awareness in their empty nature, without suppressing or correcting them.

When you do not artificially influence your mind, it is calm and clear. Therefore, leave it relaxed in its natural state, without any intention, in the open vastness of pure being.

Detach your mind from the habitual flow of thoughts so that all confusion and distraction vanish and the mind becomes silent and clear and comes to rest of its own accord.

All pleasant, neutral and unpleasant states of mind and emotions are the dynamic energy of the mind and dissolve through natural resting in pure self-awareness.

Your true essence cannot be perceived through knowledge. When all thinking and judging become silent, it is like the waves on the ocean subsiding.

The clear mind is transparent and free of illusions. It experiences the whole of existence as the one reality, which reveals itself Now-Here.

The nature of the mind and the nature of things are one. Since the light of the mind is the nature of all things, your attachment to things dissolves as soon as you perceive the true nature of your mind.

The true nature of your mind is crystal-clear awareness. Fully realising this alert, radiating awareness means liberation and a returning to your original, true essence.

Meditation makes your mind become tranquil. Through spiritual tranquillity you achieve seclusion. Through complete seclusion of the mind you enter into the innermost essence, the original Buddha-nature.

Through true insight into the original self-nature of your mind you become an enlightened being – a Buddha.

The hearts of two lovers are filled in their depths with the desire to completely dissolve into the pure love of divine essence.

Love is the yearning for oneness. Highest love aims for eternal oneness with God.

All those who have awakened to reality experienced God as light. The more you experience your true self, the more you receive divine light.

Through dedicated meditation, the ascent of the inner light is prepared until the point where, all of a sudden, it radiates forth and you experience your true self as the all-embracing eternal essence.

When your mind returns to its original state and enters into the dimension of eternity, it is completely undivided and exists of itself. Here, all misconception and ego-delusion have vanished and it experiences itself as the immortal, true self.

The realised consciousness, which has inwardly let go of itself and all things, is transformed into radiating, divine light and experiences itself as the one, immortal reality.

Translation © 2020 by John Kitching

Original title: "Die Kraft der inneren Stille"
Published by Spirit Rainbow Verlag 2020

Cover design: Michel Schmidt
Graphic design: Reinhard Zanella, Sandro Hölzel
Typesetting: Jörg Zimmermann, Torsten Zander
Inside cover photo: Axel Jung

Herstellung und Verlag:
BoD - Books on Demand, Norderstedt

ISBN 978-3-752670-55-4

Zensho W. Kopp, born 1938, is one of the most significant spiritual masters of the present and teaches a contemporary way to spiritual realisation.

The internationally renowned Zen master and author of numerous spiritual books instructs a large community of students and directs the Zen Center Tao Chan in Wiesbaden, Germany.

Tao Chan Zentrum e.V., Non-profit society, Wiesbaden

Open Zen-evening: Twice a month, the Zen Center Tao Chan in Wiesbaden organises an open Zen-evening, directed by Zen Master Zensho W. Kopp.

Information and registration: www.tao-chan.org
Visit our Facebook site at **www.facebook.com/zensho.w.kopp**.
A selection of the master's video talks can be found at **www.tao-chan.org/zen-master-zensho/videos.html**

Image credits